ISTQB Certified Tester Foundation Level Exam Practice Questions & Dumps

Exam Practice Questions for ISTQB
LATEST VERSION

Presented By: Vector Books

Copyright © 2020 by Vector Books

All rights reserved. No part of this publication may be replicated, distributed, or transmitted in any form or by any means, including photocopying, recording, or other electronic or automated methods, without the prior written consent of the publisher, except in the case of brief quotations embodied in critical reviews and certain other noncommercial uses permitted by copyright law. First Copy Printed in 2020

About Vector Books:

Vector Books is a publishing house based in Houston, Texas, USA, a platform that is available both online & locally, which unleashes the power of educational content, literary collection, poetry & many other book genres. We make it easy for writers & authors to get their books designed, published, promoted, and sell professionally on worldwide scale with eBook + Print delivery. Vector Books was founded in 2015, and is now distributing books internationally.

Note: Find answers of the questions at the last of the book.

Testlet 1

You are working as a test manager in the medical domain leading a team of system testers. You are currently working on a major release of the product which gives customers many new features and resolves a number of problem reports from previous releases.

QUESTION 1
You are about to release a test progress report to a senior manager, who is not a test specialist. Which of the following topics should NOT be included in the test progress report?

A. Product risks which have been mitigated and those which are outstanding.
B. Recommendations for taking controlling actions
C. Status compared against the started exit criteria
D. Detailed overview of the risk-based test approach being used to ensure the exit criteria to be achieved

QUESTION 2
Explain how the above mentioned report may differ from a report that you produce for the project manager, who is a test specialist Select TWO items from the following options that can be used to report to the project manager and would not be included in a report to senior management.

A. Show details on effort spent
B. List of all outstanding defects with their priority and severity
C. Give product risk status
D. Show trend analysis
E. State recommendations for release

QUESTION 3
Consider the typical objectives of testing. Which of the following metrics can be used to measure the effectiveness of the testing process in achieving one of those objectives?

A. Average number of days between defect discovery and resolution
B. Percentage of requirements covered
C. Lines of code written per developer per day
D. Percentage of test effort spent on regression testing

QUESTION 4
You have been given responsibility for the non-functional testing of a safety-critical monitoring & diagnostics package in the medical area. Which of the following would you least expect to see addressed in the test plan?

A. Availability
B. Safety
C. Portability
D. Reliability

QUESTION 5
Since the system is in the medical domain and therefore in the safety critical area, testing needs to be rigorous and evidence is required that the system has been adequately tested. Identify THREE measures that would typically be part of the test approach in this domain and which are not always applicable in other domains!

A. High level of documentation
B. Failure Mode and Effect Analysis (FMEA) sessions
C. Traceability to requirements
D. Non-functional testing
E. Master test planning
F. Test design techniques
G. Reviews

QUESTION 6
A test log is one of the documents that need to be produced in this domain in order to provide evidence of testing. However, the level of detail of test logs can vary. Which of the following is NOT an influencing factor for the level of detail of the test logs being produced?

A. Level of test execution automation
B. Test level
C. Regulatory requirements
D. Experience level of testers

QUESTION 7
Considerable attention will be given in this project to defining exit criteria and on reporting back on their status. Which combination of TWO exit criteria from the list would be best to use?

I. Total number of defects found
II. Percentage of test cases executed
III. Total test effort planned versus total actual test effort spent
IV. Defect trend (number of defects found per test run over time

A. (i) and (ii)
B. (i) and (iv)
C. (ii) and (iii)
D. (ii) and (iv)

Testlet 1

A software development organization wants to introduce some specific improvements to its test process. Currently, most of their testing resources are focussedon system testing. They are developing embedded software, and do not have a simulation environment to enable them to execute software modules on the development host. They have been advised that introducing inspections and reviews could be the most appropriate step forward.

QUESTION 1
Identify the THREE types of formal peer reviews that can be recognized.

A. Inspection
B. Management review
C. Walkthrough
D. Audit
E. Technical review
F. Informal review
G. Assessment

QUESTION 2
As part of the improvement program, the organization is also looking at tool support. Which type of tool could be used to ensure higher quality of the code to be reviewed?

A. Review tool
B. Test execution tool
C. Static analysis tool
D. Test design tool

QUESTION 3
What is the main reason why reviews are especially beneficial in the above-mentioned scenario?

A. They ensure a common understanding of the product.
B. They find defects early.
C. They enhance project communication.
D. They can be performed without exercising the code.

QUESTION 4
The introduction of reviews and inspections has often failed as a process improvement action. Identify the THREE most important measures that should be taken to reduce the risk that this test process improvement will fail.

A. Process ownership and experienced moderators who drive the inspection process.
B. Management support
C. Training of those involved
D. The availability of stands and processes
E. Usage of a more traditional software development lifecycle
F. Alignment with software process improvement
G. Using a reference model, e.g. TMMi

QUESTION 5
IEEE 1028 also defines "management review" as a type of review. What is the main purpose of a management review?

A. Align technical concepts during the design phase
B. Establish a common understanding of requirements
C. Provide independent evaluation of compliance to processes, regulations, standards etc.
D. To monitor progress, assess the status of a project, and make decisions about future actions

QUESTION 6
Which of the following is an example of testing as part of the requirements specification phase?

A. A requirements review meeting
B. A business analyst eliciting requirements
C. Performing acceptance tests against requirements
D. A test report showing requirements coverage

QUESTION 7
Which of the following is NOT a valid objective of testing?

A. Preventing defects from being introduced into the code
B. Investigating and fixing defects in the software under test
C. Gaining confidence that the system is fit-for-purpose
D. Providing information for stakeholders' decision making

QUESTION 8
During which stage of the fundamental test process is the testability of requirements evaluated?

A. Test Implementation and Execution
B. Test Planning and Control
C. Evaluating Exit Criteria and Reporting
D. Test Analysis and Design

QUESTION 9
Your company is developing a system with complex business rules and many branches in the structure of its code components. You need to choose one black box technique and one white box technique for test case design.

Which one of the following offers the BEST choice?

A. Statement testing and exploratory testing
B. Decision testing and equivalence partitioning
C. Decision testing and decision table testing
D. Boundary value analysis and decision table testing

QUESTION 10
Which one of the following statements about testing techniques is TRUE?

A. Exploratory testing can replace black box techniques when testing time is very limited
B. Test execution scheduling should give priority to experienced based testing
C. Specification based techniques can be used a substitute for a poorly defined test basis
D. Experienced based techniques are systematic and produce detailed test documentation

Testlet 1

Your company is considering whether or not to purchase a test tool suite from a respectable vendor. Your manager has searched the internet for comparable products but none of them meets his specific requirements. A tool demonstration has been arranged for next week and your team has been invited to attend. The tool suite consists of a test management tool, test execution tool and a requirements management tool. There is the possibility of adding a performance testing tool at a later stage. You have decided to attend the demo but raise some issues beforehand regarding expectations.

QUESTION 1
Select THREE issues from the options provided that should at least be raised.

A. Has there been sufficient comparison of tools?
B. What are the problems we are trying to address?
C. Do we have a set of tool requirements to validate the tool against?
D. How will the implementation be organized?
E. Which project will be selected to perform the tool pilot?
F. Is customized training available?
G. How will the change process be managed?

QUESTION 2
Which of the following would you least expect to form part of the analysis of initial tool costs?

A. Integration with other tools
B. Learning time required to use the new tool
C. Tool portability
D. Evaluation of suitable tools

QUESTION 3
A new testing tool has been selected for an organization and a pilot project has successfully completed. The next step is to deploy the tool within the organization. What is a key success factor in tool deployment?

A. Estimate a cost-benefit ratio based on a firm business case
B. Determine whether benefits will be achieved at reasonable cost
C. Provide support for the test team using the tool
D. Assessment of organizational maturity, strengths and weakness

QUESTION 4
Which of the following is a defect that is more likely to be found by a static analysis tool than by other testing techniques?

A. Omission of a major requirement
B. Inadequate decision coverage
C. Component memory leakage
D. Variables that are not used improperly declared

QUESTION 5
You are introducing a new test tool into your organization and planning a pilot project. What is a MAIN objective of this pilot project?

A. To immediately save cost for current projects in your organization
B. To show competitors that your organization is improving its test process
C. To motivate the test team and make testers feel valued
D. To learn more detail about the tool and how it fits with existing processes

QUESTION 6
A garden irrigation system allows the user to specify 2 inputs:

1. Frequency – The number of times the system should be automatically switched on per day; minimum once per day, maximum 5 times
2. Duration – The duration of operation, in whole minutes, each time it is switched on; ranging from 1 to 60

Applying 2-value boundary value analysis which of the following options has the correct test set of valid and invalid boundary values?

A. Frequency 1, 5; Duration 1, 60
B. Frequency 0, 1, 5, 6; Duration 59 seconds, 1 minute, 60 minutes, 60 minutes 1 second
C. Frequency 0, 1, 5, 6; Duration 0, 1, 60, 61
D. Frequency 0, 1, 2, 5, 6; Duration 0, 1, 30, 60, 61

QUESTION 7

	Rule 1	Rule 2	Rule 3	Rule 4	Rule 5	Rule 6	Rule 7
Conditions							
Full Member	Y	N	N	N	N	N	N
Loyalty Card holder	Don't care	Y	Y	Y	Y	N	N
18 Holes	Don't care	Y	Y	N	N	Y	N
9 Holes	Don't care	N	N	Y	Y	N	Y
Buggy/Cart Request	Don't care	N	Y	N	Y	Don't care	Don't care
Actions							
No charge on Green Fees	Y	N	N	N	N	N	N
£12 Green Fees	N	N	N	Y	Y	N	N
£16 Green Fees	N	N	N	N	N	N	Y
£18 Green Fees	N	Y	Y	N	N	N	N
£22 Green Fees	N	N	N	N	N	Y	N
Buggy/Cart allowed	Y	Y	Y	Y	Y	N	N
Buggy/Cart Free	Y	N	N	N	N	N	N
Buggy/Cart £5	N	N	Y	N	Y	N	N

The decision table above reflects a golf club's pricing structure for green fees and buggy/cart hire. What is the expected result (actions) for each of the following two test cases (TC1 and TC2)?

TC1 – Paul is not a full member, is a Loyalty Card holder and requests to play 18 holes with a buggy/cart
TC2 – Cheryl is not a full member, doesn't have a Loyalty Card and requests to play 9 holes with a buggy/cart

A. TC1 - £23 total charge including buggy hire; TC2 - £21 total charge including buggy hire
B. TC1 - £18 total charge including buggy hire; TC2 - £16 total charge including buggy hire
C. TC1 - £23 total charge including buggy hire; TC2 - £16 total charge including buggy hire
D. TC1 - £17 total charge including buggy hire; TC2 - £21 total charge including buggy hire

QUESTION 8
Which of the following activities is appropriate to the test planning stage?

A. Analyzing the test basis
B. Assigning resources for the planned activities
C. Designing the test environments
D. Writing a test execution schedule

QUESTION 9
A booking system for a city bus service prices its fares according to the time of travel:

- Peak-time tariff starts at 0600 and finishes at 1000 am Off-peak tariff
- applied during all other times of services
- The bus service does not operate between 2300 and the start of the

next day's peak service Note that all times mentioned are inclusive.

When applying the equivalence partitioning test design technique, which of the following options shows test case inputs that each fall into a different equivalence partition?

A. 0600; 1000; 1200
B. 1001; 1300; 2259

C. 0100; 0800; 2200
D. 2400, 1000, 2301

QUESTION 10

State	Events				
	A	B	C	D	E
S1	S2			S1	
S2		S3			
S3		S4	S2		
S4					S4

In the above State Table, which of the following represents an invalid transition?

A. Event C from S3
B. Event E from S4
C. Event B from S2
D. Event D from S4

QUESTION 11

	Rule 1	Rule 2	Rule 3	Rule 4	Rule 5	Rule 6
Conditions:						
Car driver	No	Yes	Yes	Yes	Yes	No
Motorcycle Driver	No	No	No	No	No	Yes
Diesel	N/A	Yes	Yes	No	No	N/A
Petrol	N/A	No	No	Yes	Yes	N/A
Engine < 1600cc	N/A	Yes	No	Yes	No	N/A
Engine > 1600cc	N/A	No	Yes	No	Yes	N/A
Actions:						
Can claim expenses	No	Yes	Yes	Yes	Yes	Yes
Expenses claim band A	N/A	Yes	No	No	No	Yes
Expenses claim band B	N/A	No	Yes	No	No	No
Expenses claim band C	N/A	No	No	Yes	No	No
Expenses claim band D	N/A	No	No	No	Yes	No

The decision table above shows a company's fuel expenses structure.

Which of the following Test Cases based on the decision table are Valid?

Test Case 1:
An employee who is not a car or motorcycle driver attempts to claim fuel expenses. Expected result: Expense claim not allowed.

Test Case 2:
An employee who drives a 1700cc diesel car attempts to claim fuel expenses. Expected result: Expense claim accepted at band C.

Test Case 3:
An employee who rides a motorcycle attempts to claim fuel expenses. Expected result: Expense claim accepted at band A.

A. Test Cases 1, 2 and 3 are all Valid.
B. Test Cases 2 and 3 are Valid. Test Case 1 is invalid.
C. Test Cases 1 and 3 are Valid. Test Case 2 is invalid.
D. Test Cases 2 is Valid. Test Cases 1 and 3 are invalid.

Testlet 1

A software development company that sells an established capture-replay tool has decided to complement it with a test management tool. The capture-replay tool was developed over a number of years and is used by a large number of clients.

The test management tool will be developed by the same team that developed the capture-replay tool, using the same technology. The company test strategy mandates that structural testing is focused at the component test level and dynamic non-functional testing is focused at the acceptance test level.

In response to growing customer demand, it is proposed to develop the test management tool in an incremental manner. Each increment will be developed using the V life cycle model. The target platform is a PC in a local area network. The PC uses a proprietary relational database and communicates with a single PC which acts as a server.

The test management tool must interface with the company s capture replay tool. Over the first 12 months of the development period the following functionality will be developed for the tool (in two increments):

basic requirements management, support for test case creation; support for test procedures, test scripts and test suites. The functionality to be included in later increments will be driven by customer demand: however, they expect to provide an incident management system, a web front-end, and interfaces to other proprietary tools and database management systems.

QUESTION 1
Which of the following are valid reasons for adopting a different life cycle (from the V model), for increments after the first year?

i. We do not have a clear understanding of the requirements from a customer perspective.
ii. We see the risk of delivering requested functionality late as being higher than the risk of delivering a lower quality product.
iii. We do not have a budget for additional regression testing which is needed to ensure that existing functionality is not compromised by future iterations.
iv. The company test strategy does not fit well within the V life cycle model.

A. (i) and (ii)
B. (i) and (iv)
C. (ii) and (iii)
D. (ii) and (iv)

QUESTION 2
Which of the following is a characteristic of good testing in any life cycle model?

A. Analysis and design of tests begins as soon as development is completed.
B. Some, but not all, development activities have corresponding test activities.
C. Each test level has test objectives specific to that level.
D. All document reviews involve the development team.

QUESTION 3
Which of the following would you expect to see in the master test plan?

A. A description of how the test cases are cross-referenced to requirements in the test management tool.

B. A detailed identification of the resources that will carry out structural testing in the first iteration.
C. The test approach that will be applied at system integration testing.
D. A list of the names of the testers who will carry out the performance testing for the final iteration.

QUESTION 4
Which of the following would be the most significant input to estimating the time to carry out the specified testing tasks?

A. The skills and experience of developers to correct the failures.
B. The standards used for the requirements specification.
C. The metrics recorded from testing the capture-replay tool.
D. The number of testers in the company and their grade.

QUESTION 5
Which of the following would be the TWO most appropriate examples of entry criteria documented in the system integration test plan?

A. The percentage of decision coverage achieved during unit testing.
B. The availability of the latest version of the capture-replay tool (for testing the interface with the newly developed test management tool).
C. The sign-off of a performance test software release note (test item transmittal report) by both development and testing showing that system performance meets the specified acceptance criteria.
D. The percentage of acceptance test procedures scheduled for execution.
E. The percentage of requirements coverage achieved during system integration test.

QUESTION 6
Which of the following type of defect would NOT be typically found by using a static analysis tool?

A. A variable is defined but is then not used
B. A variable is used in a calculation before it is defined
C. A variable has the wrong numeric value passed into it
D. A variable is used but not declared

QUESTION 7
You have been asked to improve the way test automation tools are being used in your company. Which one of the following is the BEST approach?

A. Selecting and automating scripts that test new functionality to find the most defects
B. Using a keyword-driven testing approach to separate the actions and data from the tool's script
C. Ensuring that all data, inputs and actions are stored in the tool's script for ease of maintenance
D. Keeping expected results separate from the automation tool to allow the testers to check the results

QUESTION 8
Which of the following tools would have been the MOST effective at detecting this defect prior to live implementation?

A. Dynamic analysis tool
B. Monitoring tool
C. Configuration management tool
D. Coverage measurement tool

QUESTION 9
Which of the following is a Black Box test design technique?

A. Decision Coverage
B. Error Guessing
C. Statement Coverage
D. Equivalence Partitioning

Testlet 1

The project situation after 11 months is:

- The first increment was released one week late but contained sufficient functionality to be declared fit for purpose'. However, there were 20 outstanding incidents deferred to increment two.

- The amount of voluntary overtime worked PV the test team has reduced the second Increment slippage to just 3 weeks.

- There is talk of reducing the scope of requirements. The purpose of this is to first deliver the application with support for manual testing and then to provide a delivery * weeks later to resolve any remaining points and provide support for automated testing (i.e. the link to the capture-replay tool).

- Concerns have been expressed by a section of the user community, that in some places the usability is very poor.

QUESTION 1
Which test management control option is most appropriate to adopt under these circumstances?

A. Introduce mandatory evening and weekend working to retrieve the 3 week slippage.
B. Reconsider the exit criteria and review the test plan in the context of the current situation.
C. Advise the user community regarding the reduced scope of requirements and the additional incremental delivery.
D. Arrange a meeting with the user community representatives to discuss the user interface.

QUESTION 2
Risks should be constantly reviewed. Given the current situation, which one of the following factors is most likely to lead to a revised view of product risk?

A. The concerns over the user interface may lead to changes to the interface which cannot be implemented by development in time for the second test iteration.
B. The concerns over the user interface raises the likelihood of a risk in that area and increases the amount of test effort needed for the user interface, thereby limiting the test effort available for other parts of the test management tool.

C. The delivery of the application without the interface changes may upset the user community.
D. The method used for test estimation is not accurate enough and hence the money spent on testing exceeded its budget.

QUESTION 3
Which of the following is least likely to be used as a technique to identify project and product risks?

A. Brainstorming
B. Inspections
C. Expert interviews
D. Independent assessments

QUESTION 4
Which of the following is a project risk mitigation step you might take as test manager?

A. Testing for performance problems
B. Hiring a contractor after a test analyst leaves the company
C. Arranging a back-up test environment in case the existing one fails during testing
D. Performing a project retrospective meeting using the test results after each increment

Testlet 1

You have recently been employed as a test manager for a software house producing Human Resource (HR) systems, namely Payroll, Personnel and Recruitment systems. The company is relatively new and wants to make a major impact in the market by producing a worldwide enterprise HR product.

QUESTION 1
You have been asked to write a testing strategy for the company. Which statement best explains how risk can be addressed within the testing strategy?

A. A test strategy should address identified generic product risks and present a process for mitigating those risks in line with the testing

policy.
B. A test strategy identifies the specific product for a project risk and defines the approach for the test project.
C. A test strategy is derived from the test policy and describes the way risk assessments are performed in projects.
D. A test strategy is the result of a project risk analysis and defines the approach and resources for testing.

QUESTION 2
In addition to risk, identify TWO other components of a testing strategy.

A. The entry and exit criteria for each test phase
B. Test training needs for the project resources
C. The test design techniques to be used
D. Test performance indicators
E. The test schedule

QUESTION 3
Part of the testing strategy indicates that you are going to be using systematic test design techniques. Your manager has asked that you present the main advantages of using these techniques at the next board meeting. Identify THREE main benefits of using systematic test design techniques within this company.

A. Easier to quickly adapt testing to changing requirements compared to experienced-based testing
B. Targets certain types of faults
C. Will guide experienced testers to find defects
D. Provides a way to differentiate depth of testing based on product risks by using different techniques
E. More enhanced documentation and therefore higher repeatability and reproducibility
F. Will make non-systematic testing redundant
G. Will reduce the need for early reviews

Testlet 1

For the first increment of the new enterprise HR product you have performed a product risk analysis using the FMEA method. Five risk items have been identified and the likelihood and impact have been scored using scoring tables. This has resulted in the following scores:

Risk	Likelihood	Impact
Item 1	10	2
Item 2	9	7
Item 3	7	9
Item 4	5	7
Item 5	5	5

QUESTION 1
What is the Risk Priority Number for risk item number 2?

A. 16
B. 2
C. 1
D. 63

QUESTION 2
What would be a test approach regarding the test design techniques to be applied that would fit an item with the highest risk?

A. Component testing: decision testing; System testing: exploratory testing
B. Component testing: decision testing; System testing: decision table testing
C. Component testing: statement testing; System testing: equivalence partitioning
D. Component testing: statement testing; System testing: decision table partitioning

Testlet 1

XYZ is a Swedish company and the company language is local and all system development documentation is done in the local language.

As a test manager you are currently leading an independent test team of 4 people to system test the payroll functionality. The 4 members of staff of described below:

- John is one of the senior testers. He has been working for the company the longest and has a good network of contacts. He is confident and tries to bring other team members together to promote team discussions. He is sometimes considered to be manipulative and is often seen to delegate personal work.

- Sue is a senior tester. She always seems to be busy and often seems to have too much work to do. However, she gets her work done, regardless of what it takes. She is often inclined to worry unduly and sometimes considered to be argumentative and blunt. She is conscientious and searches out errors and omissions. She always delivers on time.

- Steve is a tester. He is serious minded and often looks ahead. When he is given problems to solve he often looks at all options before deciding. He needs to be a little bit more diplomatic though in his approach to other people because his attitude often has a negative affect when trying to inspire others. He is good person discuss ideas with. Steve used to work as a business analyst on the payroll department.

- Vicki is a test analyst. She is the newest member of the team and has been employed for her automation skills. Vicki is shown to be dedicated to automation, having spent the past 5 years developing the necessary skills in automation tools. Her view on testing seems too limited; she believes automation is the only way forward.

Both John and Sue are highly experienced at finding defects based on their experience with the system and domain knowledge.

QUESTION 1
Which of the following is a benefit of independent testing?

A. Code cannot be released into production until independent testing is complete.
B. Testing is isolated from development.
C. Independent testers find different defects and are unbiased.
D. Developers do not have to take as much responsibility for quality.

QUESTION 2
A number of options have been suggested for the level of independence to be employed for the testing on the next project, and are shown below.

i. External test specialists perform non-functional testing.
ii. Testing is outsourced.
iii. Testing is carried out by the developer.
iv. A separate test team carries out the testing.
v. Testing is performed by the business.
vi. Testing is performed by a different developer.

Which of the following orders the above in a correct order of independence?

A. i, ii, iv, vi
B. ii, i, v, vi
C. ii, v, i, iii
D. i, iv, v, vi

QUESTION 3
Which of the following is a valid drawback of independent testing?

A. Developer and independent testing will overlap and waste resources.
B. Developers loose the sense of responsibility and independent testers may become a bottleneck.
C. Independent testers need extra education and always cost more.
D. Independent testers will become a bottleneck and introduce problems in incident management.

QUESTION 4
Based on the information given in the scenario, identify how the team could be improved most effectively?

A. By providing training in the payroll domain
B. By providing a workshop on test design techniques
C. By providing specific training on the systems being tested
D. By providing training on reviewing requirements

QUESTION 5
When considering the roles of test leader and tester, which of the following tasks would NOT typically be performed by a tester?

A. Prepare and acquire the test data
B. Set up and check the test environment
C. Write test summary reports
D. Review tests developed by others

QUESTION 6
What type of non-functional testing would you carry out to verify these requirements?

A. Stress testing
B. Maintenance testing
C. Load testing
D. Usability testing

Testlet 1

The project has been running for a few months and the team seems not to be progressing in their test approach. The team also lacks drive and enthusiasm and is sometimes seen to be performing their tasks too slowly. You have been asked to recruit an extra person into the team.

QUESTION 1
Which of the following team roles would be most appropriate to enhance the team and why?

A. A person with the ability to complete tasks
B. A quality assurance officer
C. A person with in-depth technical skills
D. A person who brings new ideas to the team

QUESTION 2
You are considering involving users during test execution. In general, what is the main reason for involving users during test execution?

A. They are a cheap resource
B. They have good testing skills

C. This can serve as a way to build their confidence in the system
D. They have the ability to also focus on invalid test cases

QUESTION 3
In addition to introducing the new team member, you have decided to raise motivation. Which of the measures listed below would be the best measure to take in order to increase the motivation of the team?

A. Provide more time for testing in the schedule
B. Allow people to take some time off
C. Introduce entry criteria to the testing phase
D. Organize a meeting with senior management in which they address the importance of good testing for this project

Testlet 1

Three exit criteria have been defined for the project:

- A: Test cases passed more than 70%
- B: Number of outstanding defects lest than 5
- C: Number of defects per test case less than 0.5

The first week of the testing has shown the following results:

Day	Defects Found	Defects Fixed	Tests Run	Test Passed
Monday	3	0	10	5
Tuesday	4	2	3	3
Wednesday	2	2	20	15
Tuesday	5	3	5	0
Friday	7	1	5	0

QUESTION 1
Evaluate the status of the project against the defined exit criteria. Which of the following options shows the correct status?

A. Criteria A = OK, criteria B = OK, criteria C = OK
B. Criteria A = NOT OK, criteria B = NOT OK, criteria C = OK

C. Criteria A = OK, criteria B = NOT OK, criteria C = NOT OK
D. Criteria A = NOT OK, criteria B = NOT OK, criteria C = NOT OK

Testlet 1

You have for a while been trying to hire a second test automation specialist for your test team However, you did not have any luck in finding a suitable candidate. So now, you have been asked by IT management of XYZ to forward a proposal with alternative solutions for building an automated regression test suite at system test level over a period of 2 years including needed training and eventual handover to the test team.

QUESTION 1
You have investigated different possibilities and selected four of them to present to IT management. Which of the proposals will you most likely give your highest recommendations?

A. Insourcing of test automation based on an offer from a local company ABC that has people who are specialists in system level capture-replay automation tools and they also do regular training courses in test automation methods and tools. They can then work closely with Vicki.
B. Outsourcing of test automation based on an offer from an Asian company, AsiaAutoTest, which has people who are specialists in system level capture-replay automation tools. They also offer training and besides they offer to run and maintain the regression tests in the future.
C. Internal offer from the development department of XYZ to create the regression package using CppUnit as test automation tool. One of the development groups have very good experiences in automating unit tests, and they are willing to do training as well.
D. Solution from a tool vendor offering to educate two test team members in the use of their easy-to-use test automation capture replay tool over the first 3 month and based on that build the regression test suite. In addition to Vicki, Steve is the only one that has time available to be educated.

QUESTION 2
Instead of having an independent test team within the company, the company is considering to outsource testing. What are THREE key challenges that are typical for outsourcing?

A. Test environment more complex
B. Define expectation for tasks and deliverables

C. Clear channels of communications
D. Possibly different cultures
E. Testing of non-functional requirements
F. Audit trail from requirements to test cases
G. Applying test automation

Testlet 1

You have been contracted to manage the acceptance testing of a new computer-based reservation system for a travel agency. You have provided an approximate budget estimate for the testing project based on previous experience with similar sized projects. However, the management of the parent company of the travel agency will not commit to the budget until detailed cost estimates are provided.

The reservation system is being developed by a third party However, detailed specifications of the software are available, as well as an estimate of the total effort that will be spent in developing the software. The software is to be delivered in four increments, and the functionality to be delivered in each increment has already been agreed on.

QUESTION 1
Identify THREE items that would be part of the work-breakdown structure showing the key testing activities for the acceptance test project.

A. Test planning, test case preparation and test execution for each of the four iterations
B. Work should be explicitly allocated to test completion, test management, installation and to training on using the system
C. Activities to deploy the system in the user environment
D. Regression testing in the second, third and fourth iterations
E. Development activities for unit and integration testing
F. Reviews on requirements documentation
G. Defining test environment requirements for system testing

QUESTION 2
In general which part of the testing activity is most difficult to estimate?

A. Test planning
B. Test execution
C. Test management
D. Test design

QUESTION 3
In general, why is it NOT a good idea to estimate the testing effort based only on a percentage of development effort? Identify THREE valid reasons.

A. The quality of the development estimate may be poor.
B. In general bottom-up estimation is always better than top-down estimation.
C. The percentage based technique only applies to the V life cycle model.
D. Using the same percentage every time does not address the level of risk of the application to be tested.
E. The maturity of the organization, e.g. the quality of the test basis, quality of development testing, configuration management, availability of test tools, also influence the effort needed for testing.
F. It builds on large set of historical data
G. The result is almost always a too low estimate for the required test effort

QUESTION 4
Which aspect in the test estimate is the main risk in this project?

A. Quality of the specification
B. Availability of end-users
C. The costs of hardware and tools
D. Unknown input quality due to third party development

QUESTION 5
Which of the following would be a good test technique to use when under severe time pressure?

A. Exploratory testing
B. Structure based testing
C. Specification based testing
D. Use Case testing

QUESTION 6
Which of the following options BEST explain the pesticide paradox principle of testing?

A. If we do not regularly review and revise our tests, we'll stop finding defects
B. Repeatedly running a set of tests will ensure that a system is defect free
C. Defects are, paradoxically, often contained in a small number of modules
D. Testing, like spraying pesticide, is an effective bug / defect removal activity

QUESTION 7
Testing effort can depend on a number of factors, which one of following is MOST likely to impact the amount of effort required?

A. The predicted number of defects and the amount of network required
B. The ratio of developers to testers in the project team
C. The planned use of a project management tool to schedule tasks
D. The responsibilities for testers and developers being clearly defined

Testlet 1

You have been asked to investigate various test process Improvement models to be introduced for the next project. You have been asked to provide a comparison between the TMMi and TPI models and provide a recommendation.

QUESTION 1
Model characteristics:
Which THREE of the below mentioned characteristics relate to TMMi?

A. 5 maturity levels
B. Focussed on higher level testing
C. 20 key areas
D. Highly related to CMMI
E. Continuous model
F. Staged model
G. Focussed on component and integration testing
H. Is build around 12 critical testing processes

QUESTION 2
The test improvement project will take place in an organization developing a safety-critical avionics application. Which one of the following standards do you believe would be most appropriate to take into account for compliance during your assignment?

A. ISO 9126
B. IEEE 829
C. BS 7925/2
D. DO-178B

QUESTION 3
Comparing TMMi and TPI, which is not a valid reason for choosing either TPI or TMMi?

A. If the scope of test performance improvement covers all test levels, TMMi is preferred since TPI focusses mainly on black-box testing.
B. If the organization is already applying CMMI, TMMi may be preferred since it has the same structure and uses the same terminology. TMMi addresses management commitment very strongly and is therefore more suitable to support a top-down improvement process.
C. TPI is much more a bottom-up model that is suitable for addressing test topics for a specific (test) project.
D. TMMi can only be used with the traditional V model, whereas TPI can be used with all types of software life cycles.

QUESTION 4
A test assessment has been carried out using the selected model as a reference framework. A number of recommendations have been identified and you are asked to prioritize them. Based on your knowledge of the project, you are expecting severe resistance to change. Which of the following would be the most important selection criterion for defining the priority of the recommendations?

A. Synchronized with the overall long-term organizational strategy
B. Defined according to the maturity model used
C. Most visible to stakeholders
D. Low costs actions first

QUESTION 5
Which of the following represents good testing practice for testers, irrespective of the software lifecycle model used?

A. They should start test analysis when the corresponding development level is complete
B. They should be involved in reviewing requirements or user stories as soon as drafts are available
C. They should ensure the same test objectives apply to each test level
D. They should minimize the ratio of deployment levels to test levels to reduce project costs

QUESTION 6
A system is being enhanced to simplify screen navigation for users. Which of the following does NOT reflect structural testing?

A. To test all paths that users could take through the screen menu system
B. To ensure that 100% decision testing is achieved for each system component
C. To test all branches of component calls within the application call graph
D. To ensure that users can navigate to all fields on the screen

QUESTION 7
Which of the following is a white box test technique?

A. Exploratory testing
B. Decision table testing
C. Error testing
D. Statement testing

QUESTION 8
Which of the following options describe the causal chain in the correct sequence?

A. Error, fault, failure
B. Fault, bug, mistake
C. Mistake, failure, fault
D. Failure, bug, error

QUESTION 9

Which of the following would achieve the HIGHEST level of testing independence for a project's test level?

A. Training developers to design good tests for the test team to execute
B. Outsourcing test design and execution to a different company
C. Having the company's independent test team design and execute the tests
D. Minimizing contact between testers and developers during test design to avoid bias

QUESTION 10
When can functional and structural testing BOTH be applied?

A. System and Component test levels only
B. All 'Development' test levels, i.e. those before Acceptance testing
C. Component and Component integration test levels only
D. All test levels

QUESTION 11
Which of the following options explain why it is often beneficial to have an independent test function in an organization?
A. To improve defect finding during reviews and testing
B. To ensure that developers adhere to coding standards
C. To limit communication between developers and testers
D. To provide better metrics for the stakeholders

QUESTION 12
Debugging and Testing are key activities in the software development lifecycle. Which of the following are 'Debugging' activities?

a) Identifying a failure
b) Locating the cause of failure
c) Fixing the defect
d) Checking the fix has resolved the failure

A. a & d
B. a & b
C. b & c
D. c & d

QUESTION 13
Which of the following does NOT represent one of the three triggers for maintenance testing an operational system?

A. Data migration
B. System retirement
C. System modification
D. Introduction of a test management tool

QUESTION 14
Why is measurement of code coverage important?

A. Because 100% code coverage implies 100% coverage of requirements
B. Because 100% code coverage guarantees that there are no coding errors
C. Because code coverage can be used to ensure that all code is exercised by tests
D. Because code coverage can ensure that all decisions are correctly implemented in the code

Testlet 1

You have raised the issue that improving the testing process is also dependent on the status of the software development process.

QUESTION 1
During test process improvement it is recommended to use standards where possible. Standards originate from various sources and they cover different subjects in relation to testing Pick TWO sources of software standards, useful to software testing from the ones mentioned below.

A. ISO 9126-1 'Software engineering- Product quality Part 1: Quality model' is an international standard, that provides a basis on which to define quality assurance solutions.
B. ISA 4126-1 'Software engineering- Product quality Part 1: Quality model' is an international standard, that provides a basis on which to define quality assurance solutions.
C. BS-7925-2 'Software testing. Software component testing is a national standard used internationally. It covers a number of testing techniques that may be useful both on component testing level and on system testing level.
D. SY-395-01 'Standard for East Coast Hospital software' is a regional

standard adapted from a national one. Besides hospital software, this standard ought to be used also by other types of software system in the region.

E. IEEE 829 'standard for software test documentation' is an international standard to be following mandatory by all testing origination regardless of lifecycle models.

QUESTION 2
Which of the following phases in the fundamental test process is considered to deliver a document which can be used as a major input for test process improvement?

A. Test planning and control
B. Test implementation & execution
C. Evaluating exit criteria and reporting
D. Test project closure

Testlet 1

A software house is concerned about the number of defects found in software released to its customers. They are starting to plan a new software product. In the past, releases have often been stopped due to poor planning and too many defects found during high level testing. You have been recruited to the newly created position of test manager and asked to develop a test strategy, manage the testing of the project and organize the resources needed to carry out the testing.

QUESTION 1
Which THREE activities would be valid steps during the development of the test strategy?

A. Identify test staff members that will be involved in the system test
B. Define test career paths
C. Understand the software development life cycle used by the software house
D. Assess the testing that needs to be done to minimize the risks
E. Issue the test strategy document for review
F. Define a master test plan template
G. Perform a project risk analysis

QUESTION 2
As part of the test strategy, entry and exit criteria will be defined for each test level. Which is NOT a valid reason for using entry and exit criteria?

A. The expectation is that development testing is not adequate.
B. Exit criteria are used to decide on when to stop testing.
C. Entry and exit criteria are a principal way for getting adequate resources.
D. Using entry and exit criteria will prevent software that is not or poorly tested from going to the next test level.

QUESTION 3
Within the projects, a master test plan and phase test plan will be used. Following is a list of characteristics applicable for test plans:

a) Any deviation from the procedures described in the test strategy document
b) The overall estimated costs, timescales and resource requirements
c) A detailed schedule of testing activities
d) The development deliverables to be tested
e) Which test staff members (names) will be involved and when
f) Level of requirements coverage achieved

Which THREE of the above mentioned characteristics relate to the master test plan?
A. a
B. b
C. c
D. d
E. e
F. f

QUESTION 4
Within the projects, a master test plan and phase test plan will be used. Following is a list of characteristics applicable for test plans:

a) Any deviation from the procedures described in the test strategy document
b) The overall estimated costs, timescales and resource requirements
c) A detailed schedule of testing activities
d) The development deliverables to be tested
e) Which test staff members (names) will be involved and when
f) Level of requirements coverage achieved

Which TWO of the above mentioned characteristics relate to the phase test plan?

A. a
B. b
C. c
D. d
E. e
F. f

QUESTION 5
You are examining a document which gives the precise steps needed in order to execute a test. What is the correct definition of this document?
A. Test design specification
B. Test condition
C. Test procedure specification
D. Test case specification

QUESTION 6
Which of the following would NOT be a common metric used for monitoring test preparation and execution?

A. Number of Test cases passed and failed
B. Percentage of planned test cases designed
C. Number of test plan review comments
D. Percentage of tasks complete in test environment preparation

QUESTION 7
Which of the following would you NOT expect to see on an incident report from test execution?

A. The version(s) of the software under test
B. The test execution schedule
C. Expected results and actual results
D. Precise steps to reproduce the problem

QUESTION 8
Which of the following is NOT a valid use of decision coverage?

A. Checking that all decisions have been exercised in a single program
B. Checking that all decisions have been exercised in a business process
C. Checking that all calls from one program module to another have been made correctly
D. Checking that at least 50% of decisions have been exercised by a test case suite

QUESTION 9
Which option BEST describes how the level of risk is determined?

A. The likelihood of an adverse event happening multiplied by the cost of preventing it
B. The consequences of a potential problem multiplied by the cost of possible legal action
C. The impact of an adverse event multiplied of that event occurring
D. The likelihood and the probability of a hazard occurring

Testlet 1

There is a formal requirement from the business to develop an additional on-line application to the company website which will allow existing policyholders to extend their cover for short-term foreign use of their vehicle overseas. The current manual process will be retained. The application must be implemented in months time in line with the marketing department's green initiative, which is anticipated to generate a significant increase in demand.

The development manager has insufficient resources to meet this request and has issued an invitation to potential bidders so that the development work can be outsourced.

The application must initially cover Western Europe, and later Eastern Europe, Russia, the Middle East, the Far East and Africa. A decision has yet to be made with respect to Australia, New Zealand, North and South America.
You have been asked to ensure the quality and suitability of the document sent to potential bidders and also that the application delivered by the successful bidder is 'Tit for purpose'.

QUESTION 1
Which of the following product risks would be most effectively addressed just by static testing?

A. In the delivered application, one of the countries, as specified in the requirements, has not been correctly implemented.
B. The application takes too long to process a request for additional cover.
C. The test cases do not cover the key requirements.
D. The successful bidder may not deliver all the required functionality on time.

QUESTION 2
The development manager is managing the review of the responses received from bidders, and has asked the in-house test manager to provide a review checklist for the test management aspects of the responses. Which of the following checkpoints would be appropriate?

A. The bidder's test policy should enforce that incident management fully conforms to IEEE 1044.
B. The bidder's project strategy shows that the data content of all the test environments conforms to EU standards.
C. The bidder's test plan shows that the application will be delivered for acceptance in six months time.
D. The bidder's project test plan depicts a phased implementation with later delivery dates to be confirmed and states that test deliverables will be developed using IEEE 829 as a guide.

QUESTION 3
The following Test Cases have been created for a simple web-based airline booking system.

Test Case 1: Search for an item: Available Flights Test Case 2: View selected item in My Flights
Test Case 3: Login to the system: Login is accepted
Test Case 4: Select an available flight: item added to My Flights Test Case 5: Print confirmation receipt, then exit
Test Case 6: In My Flights, confirm details and book flight

Which of the following is the correct logical order for the test cases? A. 6, 3, 1, 4, 2, 5
B. 3, 4, 1, 2, 5, 6
C. 3, 2, 1, 4, 6, 5
D. 3, 1, 4, 2, 6, 5

QUESTION 4

Your task is to compile a test execution schedule for the current release of software.

The system specification states the following logical dependencies:

- An admin user must create/amend/delete a standard user. A standard user is necessary to perform all other actions.

The test plan requires that re-tests must be performed first, followed by the highest priority tests. To save time, the test plan states that tests should be scheduled to create test data for the subsequent tests in the schedule.

The following test cases have been designed, with an indication of priority (1 being the highest priority) and whether the test has previously failed.

Id	Description	Priority	Failed
a	Log in as standard user and create customer account	2	Y
b	Order one item	3	N
c	Create invoice for order	1	Y
d	Order two items or more	3	Y
e	Log in as admin user and create a standard user	2	N

Which test execution schedule meets the test plan requirements and logical dependencies?

A. a, d, c, b, e
B. a, c, b, d, e
C. e, a, b, c, d
D. e, a, d, c, b

Testlet 1

While waiting for the responses, the test manager has been asked to prepare test plans to validate the software application delivered by the successful bidder.

QUESTION 1
Which one of the following estimation approaches is appropriate at this stage of the project?

A. Create an estimate based on the function point analysis technique and test point analysis
B. Create an estimate based on the complexity of the code
C. Create an estimate based on the credentials of the successful bidder
D. Create an estimate based on a percentage of the development effort

Testlet 1

The cancellation of a current major development project has released resources. The development manager has decided to respond to his own request to tender and has proposed an in-house development with the use of a Rapid Application Development (RAO) approach.

QUESTION 1
Why might a RAD approach be a better option for the test manager rather than a sequential development?

A. It will extend the development team's abilities and enhance future delivery capabilities.
B. It will allow the marketing, clerical and testing staff to validate and verify the early screen prototypes.
C. Time-box constraints will guarantee code releases are delivered on schedule.
D. More time can be spent on test execution as less formal documentation is required.

QUESTION 2
Which of the following is NOT a typical key challenge for testing in a RAD based development approach?

A. Re-usable test scripts for (automated) regression testing

B. Project management and control
C. No complete requirements specification
D. Time-boxing

QUESTION 3
As a result of the RAD based development approach, the test manager has decided to change the risk mitigation approach. Which test technique might be most appropriate to use?

A. Decision Table Testing
B. Boundary Value Analysis
C. Error Guessing
D. Exploratory Testing

QUESTION 4
The business has asked for a weekly progress report. Which of the following would be appropriate as a measure of test coverage?

A. Percentage of business requirements exercised
B. Percentage of planned hours worked this week
C. Percentage of countries that have test scenarios
D. Percentage of test iterations completed

Testlet 1

The following is the current incident handling process in used at the company. Step 1: Incident is documented in the incident Tile with the following information:

- Software module or area where the fault occurred
- Who has reported the fault
- Hardware configuration used for the test that found the fault
- The sequential incident number (1 greater than the last one recorded)

Step 2: Developer assigned to fix the fault Step 3: Developer fixes the fault Step 4: Developer signs off the incident as closed, and it is then removed from the incident file

QUESTION 1
Regarding the process described above, what is the most important recommendation you would make using IEEE 1044 as a guide? .

A. No priority or severity assigned
B. Incident numbering is manual rather than automated

C. No mentioning of reproduceability
D. No classification on type of incident

QUESTION 2
During the development of a software change for a system, the developer makes a mistake in his work, which leads to a fault in the code. Unfortunately, the fault is not found by software testing and is released into live.
What is the definite consequence of this mistake?

A. The system will fail, causing a defect
B. If the defect is executed, the system may fail
C. Loss of money, time, or business reputation
D. Contractual requirements have not been met by testing

Testlet 1

You are a test manager in charge of integration, system and acceptance testing for a bank. You are working on a project to upgrade an existing ATM to allow customers to obtain cash advances from supported credit cards. The system should allow cash advances from €20 to €500, inclusively, for all supported credit cards. The supported credit cards are American Express, VISA, Eurocard and Mastercard.

In the master test plan the following items are listed in the section named "items and/or features to be tested":

I All supported credit cards II Language localization
II Valid and invalid advances IV Usability
V Response time

QUESTION 1
Relying only on the information provided in the scenario, select the TWO items and/or features for which sufficient information is available to proceed with test design.

A. All supported credit cards
B. Language localization
C. Valid and invalid advances
D. Usability
E. Response time

QUESTION 2
Continuing with the Scenario described in the previous question, which of the following topics would you need to address in detail in the master test plan?

A. An approach to regression testing
B. A list of boundary values for "advance amount"
C. A description of dependencies between test cases
D. A logical collection of test cases

QUESTION 3
Given the following figures for the testing on a project, and assuming the failure rate for initial tests remains constant and that all retests pass, what number of tests remain to be run?

Test planned	1000
Initial tests run	500
Initial tests passed	350
Retests run	80

A. 700
B. 720
C. 784
D. 570

QUESTION 4
Given is the following defect removal chart reported at the end of system testing - showing total defects detected and closed defects (fixed and successfully retested). A number of open defects are classified as critical. All tests have been executed.

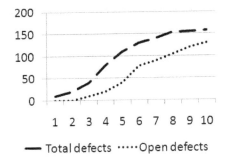

Based on the chart above, what is the most appropriate next test phase?

A. Acceptance testing to verify the business process
B. Acceptance testing to verify operational requirements
C. Requirements testing as part of testing regulatory compliance
D. Another system test cycle to verify defect resolution

Question Set 1

QUESTION 1
Which statement is most true?

A. Different testing is needed depending upon the application.
B. All software is tested in the same way.
C. A technique that finds defects will always find defects.
D. A technique that has found no defects is not useful.

QUESTION 2
The effect of testing is to:

A. Increase software quality;
B. Give an indication of the software quality;
C. Enable those responsible for software failures to be identified;
D. Show there are no problems remaining?

QUESTION 3
When is testing complete?

A. When time and budget are exhausted.

B. When there is enough information for sponsors to make an informed decision about release.
C. When there are no remaining high priority defects outstanding.
D. When every data combination has been exercised successfully.

QUESTION 4
Which list of levels of tester independence is in the correct order, starting with the most independent first?

A. Tests designed by the author; tests designed by another member of the development team; tests designed by someone from a different company.
B. Tests designed by someone from a different department within the company; tests designed by the author; tests designed by someone from a different company.
C. Tests designed by someone from a different company; tests designed by someone from a different department within the company; tests designed by another member of the development team.
D. Tests designed by someone from a different department within the company; tests designed by someone from a different company; tests designed by the author.

QUESTION 5
Which TWO of the review types below are the BEST fitted (most adequate) options to choose for reviewing safety critical components in a software project? Select 2 options.

A. Informal review.
B. Management review.
C. Inspection.
D. Walkthrough
E. Technical Review

QUESTION 6
The cost of fixing a fault:

A. Is not important
B. Increases as we move the product towards live use
C. Decreases as we move the product towards live use
D. Is more expensive if found in requirements than functional design

E. Can never be determined

QUESTION 7
Which is not the fundamental test process?

A. Planning and control
B. Test closure activities
C. Analysis and design
D. None

QUESTION 8
What is the purpose of test completion criteria in a test plan:

A. To know when a specific test has finished its execution
B. To ensure that the test case specification is complete
C. To set the criteria used in generating test inputs
D. To know when test planning is complete
E. To plan when to stop testing

QUESTION 9
Which of the following statements describes a key principle of software testing?

A. Automated tests allow better statements of confidence about the quality of software products.
B. For a software system, it is normally impossible to test all the input and output combinations.
C. Exhaustive software testing is, with enough effort and tool support, feasible for all software.
D. The purpose of software testing is demonstrating the absence of defects in software products.

QUESTION 10
Reviewing the test Basis is a part of which phase

A. Test Analysis and Design
B. Test Implementation and execution
C. Test Closure Activities

D. Evaluating exit criteria and reporting

QUESTION 11
Which of the following is a benefit of test independence?

A. It does not require familiarity with the code.
B. It is cheaper than using developers to test their own code.
C. It avoids author bias in defining effective tests.
D. Testers are better at finding defects than developers.

QUESTION 12
Failure is _____

A. Incorrect program behavior due to a fault in the program
B. Bug found before product Release
C. Bug found after product Release
D. Bug found during Design phase

QUESTION 13
Tests are prioritized so that:

A. You shorten the time required for testing
B. You do the best testing in the time available
C. You do more effective testing
D. You find more faults

QUESTION 14
Which of the following comparisons of component testing and system testing are TRUE?

A. Component testing verifies the functioning of software modules, program objects, and classes that are separately testable, whereas system testing verifies interfaces between components and interactions with different parts of the system.
B. Test cases for component testing are usually derived from component specifications, design specifications, or data models, whereas test cases for system testing are usually derived from requirement specifications, functional specifications or use cases.
C. Component testing focuses on functional characteristics, whereas system testing focuses on functional and non-functional characteristics.
D. Component testing is the responsibility of the technical testers, whereas

system testing typically is the responsibility of the users of the system.

QUESTION 15
Which of the following statements BEST describes the difference between testing and debugging?

A. Testing pinpoints (identifies the source of) the defects. Debugging analyzes the faults and proposes prevention activities.
B. Dynamic testing shows failures caused by defects. Debugging finds, analyzes, and removes the causes of failures in the software.
C. Testing removes faults. Debugging identifies the causes of failures.
D. Dynamic testing prevents causes of failures. Debugging removes the failures.

QUESTION 16
Which of the following statements BEST describes one of the seven key principles of software testing?

A. Automated tests are better than manual tests for avoiding the Exhaustive Testing.
B. Exhaustive testing is, with sufficient effort and tool support, feasible for all software.
C. It is normally impossible to test all input / output combinations for a software system.
D. The purpose of testing is to demonstrate the absence of defects. The purpose of testing is to demonstrate the absence of defects.

QUESTION 17
Which of the following could be a disadvantage of independent testing?

A. Developer and independent testing will overlap and waste resources.
B. Communication is limited between independent testers and developers.
C. Independent testers are too slow and delay the project schedule.
D. Developers can lose a sense of responsibility for quality.

QUESTION 18
Which of the following is the task of a Tester?

i. Interaction with the Test Tool Vendor to identify best ways to leverage test tool on the project.

ii. Prepare and acquire Test Data
iii. Implement Tests on all test levels, execute and log the tests.
iv. Create the Test Specifications

A. i, ii, iii is true and iv is false
B. ii, iii, iv is true and i is false
C. i is true and ii, iii, iv are false
D. iii and iv is correct and i and ii are incorrect

QUESTION 19
Which of the following is not a major task of Exit criteria?

A. Checking test logs against the exit criteria specified in test planning.
B. Logging the outcome of test execution.
C. Assessing if more tests are needed.
D. Writing a test summary report for stakeholders.

QUESTION 20
The difference between re-testing and regression testing is:

A. Re-testing is running a test again; regression testing looks for unexpected side effects
B. Re-testing looks for unexpected side effects; regression testing is repeating those tests
C. Re-testing is done after faults are fixed; regression testing is done earlier
D. Re-testing uses different environments, regression testing uses the same environment
E. Re-testing is done by developers, regression testing is done by independent testers

QUESTION 21
Non-functional system testing includes:

A. Testing to see where the system does not function properly
B. Testing quality attributes of the system including performance and usability
C. Testing a system feature using only the software required for that action
D. Testing a system feature using only the software required for that function
E. Testing for functions that should not exist

QUESTION 22
When a defect is detected and fixed then the software should be retested to confirm that the original defect has been successfully removed. This is called:

A. Regression testing
B. Maintenance testing
C. Confirmation testing
D. None of the above

QUESTION 23
Test Implementation and execution has which of the following major tasks?

i. Developing and prioritizing test cases, creating test data, writing test procedures and optionally preparing the test harnesses and writing automated test scripts.
ii. Creating the test suite from the test cases for efficient test execution.
iii. Verifying that the test environment has been set up correctly.
iv. Determining the exit criteria.

A. i, ii, iii are true and iv is false
B. i, iv are true and ii is false
C. i, ii are true and iii, iv are false
D. ii, iii, iv are true and i is false

QUESTION 24
Which of the following statements contains a valuable objective for a test team?

A. Prove that the remaining defects will not cause any additional failures.
B. Run all of the tests that are defined for the test object as quickly as possible.
C. Prove that all faults have been identified through thorough testing.
D. Cause as many failures as possible so that faults can be identified and corrected

QUESTION 25
Which of the following is MOST important in the selection of a test approach?

A. Availability of tools to support the proposed techniques.
B. The budget allowed for training in proposed techniques.
C. Available skills and experience in the proposed techniques.
D. The willingness of the test team to learn new techniques.

QUESTION 26
A deviation from the specified or expected behavior that is visible to end-users is called:

A. an error
B. a fault
C. a failure
D. a defect

QUESTION 27
According to the ISTQB Glossary, regression testing is required for what purpose?

A. To verify the success of corrective actions.
B. To prevent a task from being incorrectly considered completed.
C. To ensure that defects have not been introduced by a modification.
D. To motivate better unit testing by the programmers.

QUESTION 28
Maintenance testing is:

A. updating tests when the software has changed
B. testing a released system that has been changed
C. testing by users to ensure that the system meets a business need
D. testing to maintain business advantage

QUESTION 29
Handover of Test ware is a part of which Phase:

A. Test Analysis and Design
B. Test Planning and control
C. Test Closure Activities
D. Evaluating exit criteria and reporting

QUESTION 30
The purpose of exit criteria is:

A. Define when to stop testing
B. End of test level
C. When a set of tests has achieved a specific pre condition
D. All of the above

QUESTION 31
What is important to do when working with software development models?

A. To adapt the models to the context of project and product characteristics.
B. To choose the waterfall model because it is the first and best proven model.
C. To start with the V-model and then move to either iterative or incremental models.
D. To only change the organization to fit the model and not vice versa.

QUESTION 32
Which statement below BEST describes non-functional testing?

A. The process of testing an integrated system to verify that it meets specified requirements.
B. The process of testing to determine the compliance of a system to coding standards.
C. Testing without reference to the internal structure of a system.
D. Testing system attributes, such as usability, reliability or maintainability.

QUESTION 33
For which of the following would maintenance testing be used?

A. Correction of defects during the development phase.
B. Planned enhancements to an existing operational system.
C. Complaints about system quality during user acceptance testing.
D. Integrating functions during the development of a new system.

QUESTION 34
Reporting Discrepancies as Incidents is a part of which phase:

A. Test Analysis and Design
B. Test Implementation and execution
C. Test Closure Activities
D. Evaluating exit criteria and reporting

QUESTION 35
Important consequences of the impossibility of complete testing are:

A. We can never be certain that the program is bug free.
B. We have no definite stopping point for testing, which makes it easier for some managers to argue for very little testing.
C. We have no easy answer for what testing tasks should always be required, because every task takes time that could be spent on other high importance tasks.
D. All of the above

QUESTION 36
Which of the following is the main purpose of the component build and integration strategy?

A. to ensure that all of the small components are tested
B. to ensure that the system interfaces to other systems and networks
C. to ensure that the integration testing can be performed by a small team
D. to specify how the software should be divided into components
E. to specify which components to combine when, and how many at once

QUESTION 37
What should be the MAIN objective during development testing?

A. To cause as many failures as possible so that defects in the software are identified and can be fixed
B. To confirm that the system works as expected and that requirements have been met
C. To assess the quality of the software with no intention of fixing defects
D. To give information to stakeholders of the risk of releasing the system at a given time

QUESTION 38
Which of the following is not a part of the Test Implementation and Execution Phase?

A. Creating test suites from the test cases
B. Executing test cases either manually or by using test execution tools
C. Comparing actual results
D. Designing the Tests

QUESTION 39
Which of the following statements BEST describes one of the seven key principles of software testing?

A. Automated tests are better than manual tests for avoiding the Exhaustive Testing.
B. Exhaustive testing is, with sufficient effort and tool support, feasible for all software.
C. It is normally impossible to test all input / output combinations for a software system.
D. The purpose of testing is to demonstrate the absence of defects. The purpose of testing is to demonstrate the absence of defects.

QUESTION 40
What is the benefit of independent testing?

A. More work gets done because testers do not disturb the developers all the time.
B. Independent testers tend to be unbiased and find different defects than the developers
C. Independent testers do not need extra education and training.
D. Independent testers reduce the bottleneck in the incident management process.

QUESTION 41
What is the purpose of a test completion criterion?

A. to know when a specific test has finished its execution
B. to ensure that the test case specification is complete
C. to set the criteria used in generating test inputs
D. to determine when to stop testing

QUESTION 42
Testing should be stopped when:

A. All the planned tests have been run
B. Time has run out
C. All faults have been fixed correctly
D. Both A and C
E. It depends on the risks for the system being tested

QUESTION 43
Consider the following statements about early test design:

i. Early test design can prevent fault multiplication
ii. Faults found during early test design are more expensive to fix
iii. Early test design can find faults
iv. Early test design can cause changes to the requirements
v. Early test design takes more effort

A. i, iii & iv are true. ii & v are false
B. iii is true, i, ii, iv & v are false
C. iii & iv are true. i, ii & v are false
D. i, iii, iv & v are true, ii us false

E. i & iii are true, ii, iv & v are false

QUESTION 44
Which is not a major task of test implementation and execution?

A. Develop and prioritizing test cases, creating test data, writing test procedures and optionally, preparing test harness and writing automated test scripts.
B. Logging the outcome of test execution and recording the identities and versions of the software under test, test tools and testware.
C. Checking test logs against the exit criteria specified in test planning.
D. Verifying that the test environment has been set up correctly.

QUESTION 45
Which is not the testing objective?

A. Finding defects
B. Gaining confidence about the level of quality and providing information
C. Preventing defects.
D. Debugging defects

QUESTION 46
Which of the following is not true of regression testing?

A. It can be carried out at each stage of the life cycle.
B. It serves to demonstrate that the changed software works as intended.
C. It serves to demonstrate that software has not been unintentionally changed.
D. It is often automated.

QUESTION 47
One of the roles in a review is that of moderator, which of the following best describes this role?

A. Plans the review, runs the review meeting and ensures that follow-up activities are completed.
B. Allocates time in the plan, decides which reviews will take place and that the benefits are delivered.
C. Writes the document to be reviewed, agrees that the document can be

reviewed, and updates the document with any changes.
D. Documents all issues raised in the review meeting, records problems and open points.

QUESTION 48
What do static analysis tools analyze?

A. Design
B. Test cases
C. Requirements
D. Program code

QUESTION 49
What is the purpose of exit criteria?

A. To identify how many tests to design.
B. To identify when to start testing.
C. To identify when to stop testing.
D. To identify who will carry out the test execution.

QUESTION 50
When assembling a test team to work on an enhancement to an existing system, which of the following has the highest level of test independence?

A. A business analyst who wrote the original requirements for the system.
B. A permanent programmer who reviewed some of the new code, but has not written any of it.
C. A permanent tester who found most defects in the original system.
D. A contract tester who has never worked for the organization before.

QUESTION 51
Which of the following terms is used to describe the management of software components comprising an integrated system?

A. Configuration management
B. Incident management
C. Test monitoring
D. Risk management

QUESTION 52
For which of the following activities in the fundamental test process would an incident management tool be most useful?

A. Test planning and control
B. Test analysis and design
C. Test implementation and execution
D. Evaluating exit criteria and reporting

QUESTION 53
Which of the following defects is most likely to be found by a test harness?

A. Variance from programming standards.
B. A defect in middleware.
C. Memory leaks.
D. Regression defects.

QUESTION 54
A test management tool is most likely to integrate with which of the following tools?

A. Performance testing tool
B. Test data preparation tool
C. Static analysis tool
D. Requirements management tool

QUESTION 55
Which pair of definitions is correct?

A. Regression testing is checking that the reported defect has been fixed; retesting is testing that there are no additional problems in previously tested software.
B. Regression testing is checking there are no additional problems in previously tested software; retesting enables developers to isolate the problem.
C. Regression testing involves running all tests that have been run before; retesting runs new tests.
D. Regression testing is checking that there are no additional problems in

previously tested software, retesting is demonstrating that the reported defect has been fixed.

QUESTION 56
The following statements relate to activities that are part of the fundamental test process.

i. Evaluating the testability of requirements.
ii. Repeating testing activities after changes.
iii. Designing the test environment set-up.
iv. Developing and prioritizing test cases.
v. Verifying the environment is set up correctly.

Which statement below is TRUE?

A. (i) and (ii) are part of analysis and design, (iii), (iv) and (v) are part of test implementation and execution.
B. (i) and (iii) are part of analysis and design, (ii), (iv) and (v) are part of test implementation and execution.
C. (i) and (v) are part of analysis and design, (ii), (iii) and (iv) are part of test implementation and execution.
D. (i) and (iv) are part of analysis and design, (ii), (iii) and (v) are part of test implementation and execution.

QUESTION 57
Which of the following is true about the V-model?

A. It has the same steps as the waterfall model for software development.
B. It is referred to as a cyclical model for software development.
C. It enables the production of a working version of the system as early as possible.
D. It enables test planning to start as early as possible.

QUESTION 58
Which of the following is true of iterative development?

A. It uses fully defined specifications from the start.
B. It involves the users in the testing throughout.
C. Changes to the system do not need to be formally recorded.
D. It is not suitable for developing websites.

QUESTION 59
A top-down development strategy affects which level of testing most?

A. Component testing
B. Integration testing
C. System testing
D. User acceptance testing

QUESTION 60
Which of the following statements are true?

(i) For every development activity there is a corresponding testing activity.
(ii) Each test level has the same test objectives.
(iii) The analysis and design of tests for a given test level should begin after the corresponding development activity. (iv)Testers should be involved in reviewing documents as soon as drafts are available in the development life cycle.

A. (i) and (ii)
B. (iii) and (iv)
C. (ii) and (iii)
D. (i) and (iv)

QUESTION 61
Which of the following statements are correct for walkthroughs?

(i) Often led by the author.
(ii) Documented and defined results.
(iii) All participants have defined roles.
(iv) Used to aid learning.
(v) Main purpose is to find defects.

A. (i) and (v) are correct.
B. (ii) and (iii) are correct.
C. (i) and (iv) are correct.
D. (iii) and (iv) are correct.

QUESTION 62
Which of the following is most likely to be performed by developers?

A. Technical review of a functional specification.

B. Walkthrough of a requirements document.
C. Informal review of a program specification.
D. Static analysis of a software model.

QUESTION 63
Which of the following are most characteristic of structure-based testing?

(i) Information about how the software is constructed is used to derive test cases.
(ii) Statement coverage and/or decision coverage can be measured for existing test cases.
(iii) The knowledge and experience of people are used to derive test cases.
(iv) Test cases are derived from a model or specification of the system.

A. (i) and (ii)
B. (ii) and (iii)
C. (ii) and (iv)
D. (i) and (iii)

QUESTION 64
Which of the following are valid justifications for developers testing their own code during unit testing?

(i) Their lack of independence is mitigated by independent testing during system and acceptance testing.
(ii) A person with a good understanding of the code can find more defects more quickly using white-box techniques.
(iii) Developers have a better understanding of the requirements than testers.
(iv) Testers write unnecessary incident reports because they find minor differences between the way in which the system behaves and the way in which it is specified to work.

A. (i) and (ii)
B. (i) and (iv)
C. (ii) and (iii)
D. (iii) and (iv)

QUESTION 65
What benefits do static analysis tools have over test execution tools?

A. Static analysis tools find defects earlier in the life cycle.

B. Static analysis tools can be used before code is written.
C. Static analysis tools test that the delivered code meets business requirements.
D. Static analysis tools are particularly effective for regression testing.

QUESTION 66
Which of the following principles should be followed when introducing a test tool into an organization?
(i) Assessing organizational maturity to establish whether a tool will provide expected benefits.
(ii) Requiring a quick payback on the initial investment.
(iii) Including a requirement for the tool to be easy to use without having to train unskilled testers.
(iv) Identifying and agreeing requirements before evaluating test tools.

A. (i) and (ii)
B. (i) and (iv)
C. (ii) and (iii)
D. (iii) and (iv)

QUESTION 67
Which of the following types of test tool are most likely to include traceability functions?

(i) Performance testing tool
(ii) Requirements management tool
(iii) Configuration management tool
(iv) Static analysis tool

A. (i) and (ii)
B. (i) and (iv)
C. (ii) and (iii)
D. (iii) and (iv)

QUESTION 68
Consider the following pseudo code:

1 Begin
2 Read Time
3 If Time < 12 Then
4 Print(Time, "am")
5 Endif
6 If Time > 12 Then

7 Print(Time −12, "pm")
8 Endif
9 If Time = 12 Then
10 Print (Time, "noon")
11 Endif
12 End

How many test cases are needed to achieve 100 per cent decision coverage?

A. 1
B. 2
C. 3
D. 4

QUESTION 69
Consider the following pseudo code:

1 Begin
2 Read Time
3 If Time < 12 Then
4 Print(Time, "am")
5 Endif
6 If Time > 12 Then
7 Print(Time −12, "pm")
8 Endif
9 If Time = 12 Then
10 Print (Time, "noon") 11 Endif
12 End

If the test cases Time = 11 and Time = 15 were input, what level of decision coverage would be achieved? A. 100% or 6/6
B. 50% or 3/6
C. 67% or 4/6
D. 83% or 5/6

QUESTION 70
Given the Following program IF X <>= ZTHEN Statement 2;ENDMcCabe's Cyclomatic Complexity is :

A. 2
B. 3

C. 4
D. 5

QUESTION 71
Code Coverage is used as a measure of what?

A. Defects
B. Trends analysis
C. Test Effectiveness
D. Time Spent Testing

QUESTION 72
How many test cases are necessary to cover all the possible sequences of statements (paths) for the following program fragment?

Assume that the two conditions are independent of each other : -if (Condition 1)then statement 1else statement 2if (Condition 2)then statement 3

A. 2 Test Cases
B. 3 Test Cases
C. 4 Test Cases
D. Not achievable

QUESTION 73
To test a function, the programmer has to write a_____, which calls the function to be tested and passes it test data:

A. Stub
B. Driver
C. Proxy
D. None of the above

QUESTION 74
Boundary value testing:

A. Is the same as equivalence partitioning tests
B. Test boundary conditions on, below and above the edges of input and output equivalence classes

C. Tests combinations of input circumstances
D. Is used in white box testing strategy

QUESTION 75
Statement Coverage will not check for the following:

A. Missing Statements
B. Unused Branches
C. Dead Code
D. Unused Statement

QUESTION 76
"How much testing is enough?"

A. This question is impossible to answer
B. This question is easy to answer
C. The answer depends on the risk for your industry, contract and special requirements
D. This answer depends on the maturity of your developers

QUESTION 77
What is the concept of introducing a small change to the program and having the effects of that change show up in some test..?

A. Introducing mutations
B. Performance testing
C. A mutation error
D. Debugging a program

QUESTION 78
Which is the best definition of complete testing..?

A. You have discovered every bug in the program
B. You have tested every statement, branch, and combination of branches in the program
C. You have reached the scheduled ship date
D. You have completed every test in the test plan

QUESTION 79
Security falls under..?

A. compliance testing
B. disaster testing
C. verifying compliance to rules
D. functional testing
E. ease of operations

QUESTION 80
In the MASPAR case study..?

A. Security failures were the result of untested parts of code
B. The development team achieved complete statement and branch coverage but missed a serious bug in the MASPAR operating system
C. An error in the code was so obscure that you had to test the function with almost every input value to find its two special-case failures
D. All the above

QUESTION 81
Which is not in sequence in 11 Step Software Testing process..?

A. Assess development plan and status
B. Develop the test plan
C. Test software design
D. Test software requirement

QUESTION 82
Important consequences of the impossibility of complete testing are ..?

A. We can never be certain that the program is bug free
B. We have no definite stopping point for testing, which makes it easier for some managers to argue for very little testing
C. We have no easy answer for what testing tasks should always be required, because every task takes time that could be spent on other high importance tasks
D. All of the above

QUESTION 83
Tools like change Man, Clear case are used as..?

A. functional automation tools
B. performance testing tools
C. configuration management tools
D. none of the above

QUESTION 84
What do you mean by "Having to say NO"..?

A. No, the problem is not with testers
B. No, the software is not ready for production
C. Both a & b
D. None of the above

QUESTION 85
What are the key features to be concentrated upon when doing a testing for world wide web sites ..?

A. Interaction between html pages
B. Performance on the client side
C. Security aspects
D. All of the above

QUESTION 86
What if the project isn't big enough to justify extensive testing..?

A. Use risk based analysis to find out which areas need to be tested
B. Use automation tool for testing
C. Both a and b
D. None of the above

QUESTION 87
Faults found by users are due to..?

A. Poor quality software
B. Poor software and poor testing
C. Bad luck
D. Insufficient time for testing

QUESTION 88

When what is visible to end-users is a deviation from the specific or expected behavior, this is called..?

A. An error
B. A fault
C. A failure
D. A defect
E. A mistake

QUESTION 89

Which of the following is NOT part of configuration management..?

A. Status accounting of configuration items
B. Auditing conformance to ISO9001
C. Identification of test versions
D. Record of changes to documentation over time
E. Controlled library access

ANSWER

1) Correct Answer: D
2) Correct Answer: AB
3) Correct Answer: B
4) Correct Answer: C
5) Correct Answer: ABC
6) Correct Answer: D
7) Correct Answer: D
8) Correct Answer: ACE
9) Correct Answer: C
10) Correct Answer: D
11) Correct Answer: ABC
12) Correct Answer: D
13) Correct Answer: A
14) Correct Answer: D
15) Correct Answer: D
16) Correct Answer: D
17) Correct Answer: A
18) Correct Answer: ABC
19) Correct Answer: C
20) Correct Answer: A
21) Correct Answer: D
22) Correct Answer: D
23) Correct Answer: B
24) Correct Answer: D
25) Correct Answer: B
26) Correct Answer: B
27) Correct Answer: C
28) Correct Answer: A
29) Correct Answer: A
30) Correct Answer: C
31) Correct Answer: C
32) Correct Answer: C
33) Correct Answer: AB
34) Correct Answer: C
35) Correct Answer: A
36) Correct Answer: A
37) Correct Answer: D
38) Correct Answer: B

39) Correct Answer: B
40) Correct Answer: B
41) Correct Answer: C
42) Correct Answer: A
43) Correct Answer: AC
44) Correct Answer: BDE
45) Correct Answer: D
46) Correct Answer: B
47) Correct Answer: C
48) Correct Answer: B
49) Correct Answer: B
50) Correct Answer: B
51) Correct Answer: D
52) Correct Answer: D
53) Correct Answer: D
54) Correct Answer: C
55) Correct Answer: D
56) Correct Answer: B
57) Correct Answer: A
58) Correct Answer: BCD
59) Correct Answer: ABD
60) Correct Answer: B
61) Correct Answer: ADE
62) Correct Answer: D
63) Correct Answer: A
64) Correct Answer: C
65) Correct Answer: C
66) Correct Answer: ADF
67) Correct Answer: D
68) Correct Answer: D
69) Correct Answer: C
70) Correct Answer: D
71) Correct Answer: C
72) Correct Answer: D
73) Correct Answer: A
74) Correct Answer: A
75) Correct Answer: D
76) Correct Answer: D
77) Correct Answer: C
78) Correct Answer: A
79) Correct Answer: A
80) Correct Answer: AC